First published in this format 2015

Text: Stephanie Dosen
Jacket/Interior Design: Kimberly Adis
Photographer: Simon Raymonde
Editor: Tim Stobierski
Copy Editor: Betty Christiansen

The Taunton Press
Inspiration for hands-on living®

The Taunton Press, Inc.
63 South Main Street
PO Box 5506, Newtown
CT 06470-5506
e-mail: tp@taunton.com

Threads® is a trademark of The Taunton Press, Inc., registered
in the U.S. Patent and Trademark Office.

The following names/manufacturers appearing in *Forest
Fairytale Knits* are trademarks: Jo-Ann Fabric and Craft
Stores®, Michaels®

Library of Congress Cataloging-in-Publication Data

Dosen, Stephanie.
  Forest fairytale knits : 7 enchanting projects to make & share /
Stephanie Dosen of tiny owl knits.
    pages cm. -- (Threads selects)
  ISBN 978-1-63186-326-4
  1. Knitwear. 2. Knitting--Patterns. I. Title.
  TT825.D67 2015
  746.43'2--dc23
                    2015019611

Printed in the United States of America
10 9 8 7 6 5 4 3 2 1

TABLE OF
CONTENTS

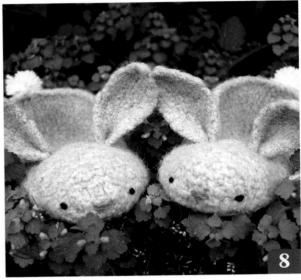

orchids & fairy lights winter hat

magic treetop book bag

sleeping beauty cowl

INTRODUCTION

HELLO, LOVELIES!

THANK YOU SO MUCH FOR KNITTING WITH ME ON A FOREST STROLL THOUGH A FIBER TALE! I'll be with you as you walk through these pages and learn how to make pretty things out of sticks and strings. What magic! Like every good fairy tale, this booklet will teach you the secrets to age-old questions such as "Which hat is best to wear while walking my bunny?" and "What should I wear if invited to the cottage of the Brothers Grimm?" I'LL BE WITH YOU TO OFFER TIPS AND ADVICE AS YOU GO, so you won't be alone on your journey through the woolly wilderness.

One of the biggest concerns I hear from knitters all over the world is that they are afraid that knitting patterns might be scary! They say to me over and over, "Oh, I can't do that! That looks too hard." I'M HERE TO ENCOURAGE YOU TO KNIT BRAVELY, DEAR KNITTER. You can do it! I promise you that these patterns won't bite like the big bad wolf; they will only keep you warm and happy. All knitting happens one tiny step at a time. So let's knit wildly and madly, and when we mess up (we all do), we can just rip back a little and start again. It's all part of the tale. Like every good story, your knitting projects will have a happy ending. As you go forth, good knitter, remember to BE AFRAID OF LIONS AND BEARS, BUT NEVER, EVER BE AFRAID OF YOUR KNITTING!

HAPPILY EVER AFTER YOURS TRULY,

Stephanie xoxo

GRIMM'S COTTAGE

Put on your capelet my dear! We are going to sit by the fire in the cottage of the Brothers Grimm. They have many stories to tell. We shall stay awake into the night until we've heard every wild, magical, adventurous tale.

experience level
Intermediate

size
S/M: Bust size 32–38

L/XL: Bust size 40–46, L/XL directions in ( ).

measurements
Measured flat

S/M: 20 in. wide at base, 21 in. from top to bottom

L/XL: 25 in. wide at base, 26 in. from top to bottom

Note: When measured flat, ribbing takes the capelet in a lot. It will stretch and has quite a bit of ease and give.

yarn
Approx 260 (435) yd. super bulky wool yarn (CYCA 6)

shown in
Rowan Big Wool: 100% merino wool (87 yd./80 m, 3.5 oz./100 g), 3 (5) balls #61 Concrete

gauge
9 sts = 4 in. in St st using U.S. size 15 (10 mm) needles

notions
• One U.S. size 15 (10 mm) circular needle, 16 in. long (or size necessary for gauge)
• One U.S. size 15 (10 mm) circular needle, 24 in. long (or size necessary for gauge)
• One U.S. size 15 (10 mm) dpns (or size necessary for gauge; used for the gauntlets)
• Stitch markers
• Tapestry needle
• 8 (11) yd. ribbon

Consider using strips of fabric instead of ribbon.

tiny owl stitch guide
See p. 30 for abbreviations.

to make the capelet
With size 15 16-in. circular needle, loosely CO 42 (48) sts, join in the round, and pm. Slip marker when it is reached at the end of each round.

Round 1: *K1, p2; rep from * to end.

Work Round 1 a total of 16 times.

Round 17: *Kfb, p2; rep from * to end. 56 (64) sts.

Round 18: *K1, p3; rep from * to end.

Round 19: Rep Round 18.

Round 20: *Kfb, p3; rep from * to end. 70 (80) sts.

Round 21: *K1, p4; rep from * to end.

Round 22: Rep Round 21.

Round 23: *Kfb, p4; rep from * to end. 84 (96) sts.

Round 24: *K1, p5; rep from * to end.

Round 25: Rep Round 24.

Round 26: Yo, k1 (mark this knit st with a marker or pin), yo, p41 (47), yo, k1 (mark this knit st also), yo, purl to end of round.

Round 27: Purl all sts except 2 marked knit sts, knit those.

Note: Each time you knit a marked st, you may want to move marker up to the new knit st made to keep better track of them as you go along.

Round 28: *Purl and stop before marked st, yo, k marked st, yo, rep from * then purl to end of round.

Work Rounds 27 and 28 1(2) more time(s). 96, (112) sts.

Work Round 27 one more time.

Note: Leave your stitch markers in for now.

Round 30 (both sizes): Purl all sts, meanwhile: K.

S/M: Make 2 increases during this round. (Use m1p to make increases and try to space them out somewhat evenly.)

L/XL: Make no increases during this round, just purl all sts.

You should now have 98 (112) sts.

Remove beginning-of-round marker and set it aside; now purl and stop right after you've purled the marked st.

Replace marker here. (This is the new round beginning.)

Begin eyelet rib pattern.

Note: You can take out the 2 knit stitch markers now, but leave the beginning-of-round marker in.

eyelet rib
(This pattern is a multiple of 7 sts)

Round 1: * K5, p2; rep from * to end.

Round 2: Rep Round 1.

Round 3: * K2tog, yo, k1, yo, skp, p2; rep from * to end.

Round 4: Rep Round 1.

Work Rounds 1–4 of eyelet rib for a total of 9 (13) times. Then work Rounds 1 and 2 again and bind off in pattern.

Weave your first eyelet ribbon before pre-cutting all of your ribbon. You'll have enough to make each ribbon approx 33 (43) in. long.

ribbons

To start, weave a ribbon through an eyelet at the top of the capelet and tie it in a bow. Then, weave tails down by going in and out of the eyelets. Work every other row this way.

Tie ends in a knot on the other side.

to make the gauntlets
(Make 2)

Using size 15 dpns, cast on 17 (20) sts and join in the round. Knit 20 rounds. Bind off.

Now you know just what to wear when you visit the cottage of the Brothers Grimm. They will tell you billions of wild tales while you are there, so it is best to stay warm while you listen.

HOPSALOTS

What bedroom is complete without a pair of li'l bunny slippers poking out from under the bed? Hopsalots will help you with all sorts of things, like hopping and dusting and stuff.

experience level
Intermediate

sizes
Womens S: U.S. 5–6

Womens M: U.S. 7–8

Womens L: U.S. 9–10
Instructions included for more toe room for wide feet.

measurements
• Slippers are felted to fit your foot.

• Pre-felted, seamed sole measures 11 (12, 13) in. long.

yarns
Approx 440 yd. DK weight wool yarn (CYCA 3), held doubled

shown in
Sirdar Eco Wool: 100% undyed wool (109 yd./100 m, 1.75 oz./50 g), 4 balls #201 Natural

gauge
12 sts and 16 rows = 4 in. in St st using U.S. size 11 (8 mm) needles with yarn held doubled.

notions
• One pair U.S. size 11 (8 mm) straight needles 10 in. long (or size necessary for gauge)

• Tapestry needle

• Stitch markers

• Scraps of red and black fingering yarn for eyes and nose

• Scraps of white angora yarn for pom-pom tails

• Needle and thread

tiny owl stitch guide
See p. 30 for abbreviations.

PATTERN NOTES
Hopsalots are knitted flat and seamed up. So simple! Use DK weight yarn held doubled for slippers.

to make slipper body

With yarn held doubled and size 11 needles, CO 28 sts.

Knit 3 rows. (Yup, that's good ol' garter st.)

Note: From now on, as you go, slip 1st st of each row; on RS rows slip knitwise, and on WS rows, grab back of the st and slip purlwise.

Row 4 (WS): P9, pm, k10, pm, p9.

Row 5 (RS): Knit.

Rep Rows 4 and 5, slipping markers as you go, until work is a total of 26 (30, 34) rows, approx 6½ (7½, 8½) in. from CO.

Next RS row, begin decreases as follows:

Row 1 (RS): Ssk, knit to last 2 sts, k2tog.

Row 2 (WS): Purl to marker, k10, purl to end.

Rep rows 1 and 2, slipping markers until 4 sts rem.

Note: Remove markers once you have decreased past them. From that point on, simply work your Row 2 as a knit row.

Next RS row, begin increases for top of toe as follows:

Note: You can stop slipping the 1st sts of every row now.

Row 1: K1, m1, knit to last st, m1, k1.

Row 2: Knit.

Rep Rows 1 and 2 until you have 14 sts.

If you have wide feet, go until you have 16 sts.

Next RS row, begin decreases as follows:

Row 1: Ssk, knit to last 2 sts, k2tog.

Row 2: Knit.

Rep Rows 1 and 2 until 4 sts rem.

Next RS row: K2tog, k2tog, pass 1st st over next st, break yarn, and pull through loop. Weave end.

to make ears
(Make 4)

Note: Pre-felted ear is about 5 in. high.

With yarn held doubled and size 11 needles, CO 7 sts.

Starting with a purl row, work in St st for 13 rows.

Row 14 (RS): Ssk, knit to last 2 sts, k2tog.

Row 15: Purl.

Rep Rows 14 and 15 until 3 sts rem.

Next RS row: Slip 1, k2tog, pass 1st st over next st, break yarn, and weave end.

Seaming the heel.

Felt and shape ears separately and attach last. Ears are important because bunnies like to hear all the good gossip. They've also been known to watch a soap opera or two.

Before and after felting.

to seam the heel and toe

Heel: Fold the slipper in half lengthwise with wrong sides facing. Seam up the entire length of heel using whipstitch. Extend the seam to include a few sts over the top of heel. Toe: Fold the diamond-shaped toe back and whipstitch all the way around it, attaching it to the body of foot.

Note: Seams will completely disappear when they felt, so go ahead and seam these up like a five-year-old might. It won't matter!

to felt

I prefer hand felting to washing-machine felting. That way, I can monitor the progress and mold and shape along the way. Plus, it's just good fun! Drench slippers in hot water and add a bit of soap (try lavender or patchouli). Squeeze water out. Rub slippers this way and that vigorously for about 30 minutes. Just when you think they are never going to felt, they suddenly will. Magic!

Note: Don't forget to rinse out all of the soap before shaping.

While slippers are still damp, begin shaping. Try them on throughout the process to ensure proper length. There will be a minute where they look insanely wrong. Don't fret! Be patient and mold them like clay to your foot. I had a jagged spot in one of mine, so I just made a stitch and felted it in. Shape the toe using your rounded fist. Set them out to dry in the shape you'd like them to retain.

finishing

Note: Work when everything is dry.

Ears: With needle and thread, use a stitch to pinch the base of each ear closed, then stitch the ears to the head.

Nose: Thread a needle with red fingering yarn held quadrupled. Run a ¼-in. horizontal stitch across the front. Easy!

Eyes: Thread a needle with black fingering yarn held quadrupled. Run a tiny ⅛-in. horizontal stitch for each eye. Puff up.

Tail: Make a tiny 1-inch pom-pom using white angora yarn.

Hop it! Bunnies need lots of rest, so make sure you put your feet up a lot.

MOSS & BLUEBELLS

This mossy scarf has little pockets hidden in the bluebells.
Put your hands inside if they get chilly, or fill them with
forest flowers and kittens on your walk.

experience level
Intermediate

size
One size

measurements
- Finished length, including pockets: about 71 in.
- Scarf width: 4 in.
- Pocket width: 4½ in., measured flat.

yarn
Approx 580 yd. DK weight yarn (CYCA 3)

shown in
The Fibre Company Acadia: 60% merino, 20% silk, 20% alpaca (145 yd./133 m, 1.75 oz./50 g), 2 skeins Asparagus (MC) and 2 skeins Sea Lavender (CC).

gauge
22 sts = 4 in. in St st using U.S. size 6 (4 mm) needles

notions
- One U.S. size 6 (4 mm) circular needle 16 in. long (or size necessary for gauge)
- Stitch marker
- Tapestry needle

tiny owl stitch guide
See p. 30 for abbreviations.

PATTERN NOTES
Oh, I love pocket scarves. Don't you? The moss scarf and bluebell pockets are knitted separately and then seamed together at the end. Easy!

to make bluebell pockets
(Make 2)

Note: Start at the bottom and knit in the round. You'll seam the bottom of the pockets closed later.

With CC and size 6 needle, loosely CO 40 sts, pm, and join in the round. If the sts are too tight to fit around needle, you could start these on dpns, but keep it loose.

Set-up Rounds: Purl 2 rounds.

Round 1: * P4, CO 8 sts (see Tiny Owl Stitch Guide on p. 30 for help casting on in the middle of a row); rep from * to end.

Round 2: * P4, k8; rep from * to end.

Round 3: * P4, ssk, k4, k2tog; rep from * to end.

Round 4: * P4, k6; rep from * to end.

Round 5: * P4, ssk, k2, k2tog; rep from * to end.

Round 6: * P4, k4; rep from * to end.

Round 7: * P4, ssk, k2tog; rep from * to end.

Round 8: * P4, k2; rep from * to end.

Round 9: * P4, k2tog; rep from * to end.

Round 10: * P4, k1; rep from * to end.

Round 11: * P3, p2tog; rep from * to end.

Work Rounds 1–11 a total of 5 times.

Rib Round: * K2, p2; rep from * to end.

Work Rib Round a total of 3 times and BO in rib pattern. Break yarn, weave end, and set pockets aside.

to make moss scarf

Note: This section is knit flat and separately.

With MC and size 6 needles, CO 23 sts.

Row 1 (RS): K1, p3, * keep yarn at front of work and slip 3 sts purlwise, p3; rep from * to last st, k1.

Row 2: P1, k3, * keep yarn at back of work and slip 3 sts purlwise, k3; rep from * to last st, p1.

Row 3: K1, p3, * k3, p3; rep from * to last st, k1.

Row 4: P1, k3, * p3, k3; rep from * to last st, p1.

Row 5: K5, * pull up loop (see Tiny Owl Stitch Guide on p. 30 for instructions on pulling up loop), k5; rep from * to end.

Row 6: K1, p3, * k3, p3; rep from * to last st, k1.

Row 7: P1, *keep yarn at front of work and slip 3 sts purlwise, p3; rep from * to last 4 sts, keep yarn at front of work and slip 3 sts purlwise, p1.

Row 8: K1, *keep yarn at back of work and slip 3 sts purlwise, k3; rep from * to last 4 sts, keep yarn at back of work and slip 3 sts purlwise, k1.

Row 9: P1, k3, * p3, k3; rep from * to last st, p1.

Row 10: K1, p3, * k3, p3; rep from * to last st, k1.

Row 11: K2, * pull up loop, k5; rep from * to last 3 sts, pull up loop, k2.

Row 12: P1, k3, * p3, k3; rep from * to last st, p1.

Repeat Rows 1–12 for 54 in. or desired length. Bind off.

assembly

First, block moss scarf to help it stay nice and flat.

Thread a tapestry needle with CC and seam the bottom of your bluebell pockets closed using your preferred stitch.

Thread a tapestry needle with CC and stitch the inside of the opening of each pocket to each end of the RS of the moss scarf. I used a simple whipstitch and then wove the end down into the bluebells. It doesn't have to be perfect.

There are lots of uses for the pockets, but consider stashing a few granola bars in case you run in to any hungry forest bears.

SHIPS & SEASIDE

Let's go down to the seaside and watch the ships! Big wool blanket? Check. Big basket full of bread and berries? Check. Storybooks for reading aloud? Check. Cozy seaside cowl with lots of stripes? Oh, yes, please!

experience level
Beginner

size
One size

measurements
When worn, cowl sits about 14 in. tall on your neck and has a circumference of about 31 in.

yarn
Approx 918 yd. Aran weight kid mohair (CYCA 4)

shown in
Rowan Kid Classic: 70% lamb's wool, 26% kid mohair, 4% nylon (153 yd./ 140 m, 1.75 oz./50 g), 2 balls #851 Straw (Color A–tan), 2 balls #865 Dashing (Color B–grey), 1 ball #866 Bitter Sweet (Color C–brown), 1 ball #856 Tattoo (Color D–teal)

gauge
18 sts = 4 in. in St st using U.S. size 8 (5 mm) needles

notions
- One U.S. size 8 (5 mm) circular needle, 24 in. or 16 in. (or size necessary for gauge)
- Stitch markers
- Crochet hook for provisional cast-on
- Tapestry needle
- Spare circular needle to hold sts while working Kitchener st (any size near U.S. 8 will do)

tiny owl stitch guide
See p. 30 for abbreviations.

Have lots of fun at the seaside wearing your new cowl! Be sure to collect lots of pretty shells and stones. Then, make wishes on them and toss them back into the water for luck!

PATTERN NOTES

This cowl is just like an inner tube. It begins with a provisional cast-on. Then, a tube is knitted in the round in the stripe sequence. Finally, the provisional cast-on is removed and the two live edges are seamed together using Kitchener stitch. Yeah, it's a little buggy to work such a long row of Kitchener stitch, I agree, but once it's finished, you have a never-ending, no-edged, magical "inner tube-like" cowl with no seams or wrong sides. Wear it any which way you like; there isn't a bad side!

to knit cowl

With size 8 circular needle and Color B, and using the provisional cast-on method of your choice (I prefer to crochet a loose chain and pick up into the back bump of the chain), CO 127 sts. Join in the round and place marker. Now work stripe sequence while knitting every round of the tube.

Stripe sequence:

2 rounds Color B

2 rounds Color A

2 rounds Color B

2 rounds Color A

2 rounds Color B

20 rounds Color A

1 round Color D

2 rounds Color A

1 round Color D

2 rounds Color A

1 round Color D

2 rounds Color A

1 round Color D

10 rounds Color A

1 round Color C

10 rounds Color A

1 round Color D

2 rounds Color A

1 round Color D

2 rounds Color A

1 round Color D

2 rounds Color A

1 round Color D

15 rounds Color A

2 rounds Color B

2 rounds Color A

2 rounds Color B

2 rounds Color A

20 rounds Color B

1 round Color A

10 rounds Color B

1 round Color C

2 rounds Color B

1 round Color C

2 rounds Color B

1 round Color C

10 rounds Color B

1 round Color A

10 rounds Color B

1 round Color C

2 rounds Color B

1 round Color C

2 rounds Color B

1 round Color C

10 rounds Color B

1 round Color A

11 rounds Color B

After stripe sequence, tube should measure approx 31 in. long. If it doesn't, add some extra rows in Color B. Break yarn leaving a long tail for Kitchener stitch. (The tail needs to be long enough to knit another round.)

seaming with kitchener stitch

Remove provisional cast-on carefully and place live sts on a spare circular needle. Make sure that the points of both sets of circular needles match up.

Fold edges in and get ready to work Kitchener st to seam the 2 live edges together. You might want to make some tea.

Align your work so both sets of needles are pointing to the right and your tail is coming off of back needle. Thread a tapestry needle and work Kitchener st as foll:

Q: Oh before I start, how loose should my Kitchener stitch row be?

A: *Good question. The Kitchener stitch row should look just like a row of knitted stitches. If you are nervous about it, keep it loose at first. You can always go back and tighten the row to the correct tension when you are finished.*

Kitchener stitch set-up
Go into 1st st on needle closest to you as if to purl. Leave st on needle.

Go into 1st st on needle farthest from you as if to knit. Leave st on needle. This sets up your seam.

Kitchener stitch
Front needle
Go into 1st st knitwise. Slip st off needle.

Go into next st purlwise. Leave st on needle.

Back needle
Go into 1st st purlwise. Slip st off needle.

Go into next st knitwise. Leave st on needle.

Rep these 4 rows until all sts are worked. Weave in end and go back to tighten any loose sts if necessary.

WINTER HAT

ORCHIDS & FAIRY LIGHTS

This slouchy hat is decked with fairy lights. It's perfect for wandering, train travel, and walking your bunny.

experience level
Intermediate

size
One size

yarn
Approx 210 yd. worsted weight yarn (CYCA 4)

shown in
Malabrigo Merino Worsted: 100% merino wool (210 yd./192 m, 3.5 oz./100 g), 1 skein #34 in Orchid

gauge
18 sts = 4 in. in St st using U.S. size 7 (4.5 mm) needle

notions
- One U.S. size 7 (4.5 mm) circular needle 16 in. long (or size necessary for gauge)
- One set U.S. size 7 (4.5 mm) dpns (or size necessary for gauge)
- Stitch marker
- Cable needle
- Tapestry needle

tiny owl stitch guide
See p. 30 for abbreviations.

to begin hat
With size 7 needle, cast on 80 sts, pm, and join in the round. Slip marker when you come to it at the end of each round and switch to dpns when necessary.

Rib Round: *K1, p1; rep from * to end.

Rep Rib Round for 1 in.

Next round: M1,*k3, m1; rep from * to last 2 sts, k1, m1, k1. 108 sts.

Set-up Round: *P5, k2, p5 rep from * to end.

Note: Take extra care to note the placement of the * in set-up round.

21

to knit orchids and fairy lights

(10-round pattern)

Round 1: *P5, k2, p5; rep from * to end.

Round 2: *P4, c2b, c2f, p4; rep from * to end.

Round 3: *P3, t2b, k2, t2f, p3; rep from * to end.

Round 4: *P2, t2b, c2b, c2f, t2f, p2; rep from * to end.

Round 5: *P1, t2b, p1, k4, p1, t2f, p1; rep from * to end.

Round 6: *T2b, p1, t2b, k2, t2f, p1, t2f; rep from * to end.

Round 7: *K1, p2, k1, p1, k2, p1, k1, p2, k1; rep from * to end.

Round 8: *Mb, p1, t2b, p1, k2, p1, t2f, p1, mb; rep from * to end.

Round 9: *P2, k1, p2, k2, p2, k1, p2; rep from * to end.

Round 10: *P2, mb, p2, k2, p2, mb, p2; rep from * to end.

Rep Rounds 1–10 3 more times. (Total of 4 times.)

to knit decreases

Note: Switch to dpns when necessary.

Round 1: P3, p2tog, k2, *p8, p2tog, k2; rep from * around, end p5.

Round 2: P2, p2tog, k2, *p7, p2tog, k2; rep from *, end p5.

Round 3: P1, p2tog, k2, *p6, p2tog, k2; rep from *, end p5.

Round 4: P2tog, k2, *p5, p2tog, k2; rep from *, end p4, p2tog. Remove marker so you can work p2tog. Replace it again after p2tog.

Round 5: *K2, p4, p2tog; rep from * around, end k2, p3, p2tog.

Round 6: *K2, p3, p2tog; rep from * around, end k2, p2, p2tog.

Round 7: *K2, p2, p2tog; rep from * around, end k2, p1, p2tog.

Round 8: *K2, p1, p2tog; rep from * around, end k2, p2tog.

Round 9: *K2, p2tog; rep from * around, k2, k2tog. (You'll have to remove your marker again so just leave it out now.)

Round 10: [K2tog, k1] 8 times, k1. 18 sts.

Break yarn and thread through live sts with tapestry needle. Weave ends in securely.

Now you have the perfect slouchy hat to wear for everyday slouchy joy! You will find it is the perfect thing to wear for collecting pinecones, eating ice cream, and walking your bunny.

BOOK BAG

MAGIC TREETOP

Magic Treetop Book Bag is the perfect size for stashing away
your newest library finds! Take it to the nearest tree
and let it swing from a branch as you read the day away.

experience level
Intermediate

size
One size

measurements
• After felting: 14 in. wide and 10 in. tall
• Felted and twisted strap is about 25 in. long

yarn
Approx 225 yd. super bulky wool yarn (CYCA 6)

shown in
Blue Sky Alpacas Bulky Natural:
50% alpaca 50% wool (45 yd./41 m, 3.5 oz./100 g), 5 skeins #1002 Silver Mink

gauge
8 sts = 4 in. in St st using U.S. size 17 (12 mm) needles before felting

notions
• One U.S. size 15 (10 mm) circular needle 24 in. long
• One pair U.S. size 17 (12 mm) straight needles (or size necessary for gauge)
• One 1½-in. button (it's not functional so use any size)
• Crochet hook for attaching fringe
• Tapestry needle

tiny owl stitch guide
See p. 30 for abbreviations.

Drop the markers. Hold bag so the needles are pointing toward your right hand and the yarn is coming off the needle farthest from you.

Break yarn, leaving a tail that is long enough to knit a row, thread it with a tapestry needle, and work Kitchener st:

Kitchener stitch set-up
Go into 1st st on needle closest to you as if to purl. Leave st on needle.

Go into first st on needle farthest from you as if to knit. Leave st on needle. This sets up your seam.

Kitchener stitch
Front needle
Go into 1st st knitwise. Slip st off needle.

Go into next st purlwise. Leave st on needle.

Back needle
Go into 1st st purlwise. Slip st off needle.

Go into next st knitwise. Leave st on needle.

Rep these 4 rows until all sts are worked. Weave in end. Woo yay! The bag part is done!

Owlie note about Kitchener stitch
Don't pull too tightly when you are working your Kitchener stitch. Stop pulling when the seam looks just like another row of stitches. If done correctly, the Kitchener stitch should look just like a row of stitches. Cool!

PATTERN NOTES
Magic Treetop Book Bag is knitted in the round. The bottom is then seamed using Kitchener stitch. The flap is picked up and knitted last.

to make the bag
With size 15 circular needle, cast on 54 sts, join in the round and pm. Knit 1 round.

Next round: *K6, m1; rep from * 63 sts to end.

Next round: K3, m1, knit the rest of the round. 64 sts.

Cont in St st. until piece measures 11 in. Now stop 2 sts before marker. Work decrease rounds as follows:

Round 1: Ssk, sm, k2tog, k28, ssk, pm, k2tog, knit to 2 sts before marker, ssk.

Round 2: K2tog, k26, ssk, sm, k2tog, knit to 2 sts before marker, ssk.

Round 3: K2tog, k24, ssk, sm, k2tog, knit to 2 sts before marker, ssk.

Round 4: K2tog, k22, ssk, sm, k2tog, knit to end. 48 sts.

seaming the bottom with kitchener stitch
Divide sts evenly at the markers onto 2 long straight or circular needles (24 sts per needle) with points facing toward working yarn. Use any size needle between a U.S. 10–15 for this, as they are just holding the sts while you seam.

flap

With size 17 needles and right side facing, pick up and knit 27 sts along one side of the opening edge. When you pick up, go into the farthest outside loop of your CO. Turn.

Starting with a purl row, work St st for 11 in.

Next knit row, begin decreases as follows:

Row 1: Ssk, knit to end of row.

Row 2: Purl.

Row 3: [Ssk] 4 times, knit to end of row.

Row 4: Purl.

Row 5: [Ssk] 4 times, knit to end of row.

Row 6: Purl to last 4 sts, p2tog, p2tog.

Row 7: [Ssk] twice, knit to end of row.

Row 8: Purl to last 2 sts, p2tog.

Row 9: [Ssk] twice, knit to last 2 sts, k2tog.

Row 10: Purl.

Row 11: [Ssk] twice, knit to end of row.

Row 12: Purl to last 2 sts, p2tog.

Row 13: Ssk, knit to end of row.

Row 14: Purl.

Row 15: [K2tog] twice, slip the 1st st over the next and pull yarn through. Cut yarn to 4 in. and let it hang (this will be part of the fringe).

strap

With size 17 needles, CO 2 sts and work I-cord for 90 in. Need help with an I-cord?

I-cord extravaganza
1. CO 2 sts. It's best to work an I-cord on dpns, but I've included instructions for circular and straight needles too.

2. Knit 2 sts. Do not turn work. Keep front facing and slide work to the other end of your dpn.

Note: If you are on circular needles, just slide it all the way down your circular needle until it reaches the tip of the other needle. If you are on straight needles, just slip the 2 sts back onto the needle in your left hand purlwise.

3. The stitches are ready to knit again, but your yarn is on the wrong side. That's okay! Bring the yarn behind the work (snug but not too snug) and knit 2 sts again. Cont to work in this manner for 90 in.

Rep steps 1–3 for 90 in. Break yarn and weave through live stitches, cinching them closed.

leaf

With size 15 needles, leave a 6-in. tail and CO 3 sts.

Row 1 and all odd rows: Purl.

Row 2: K1, yo, k1, yo, k1.

Row 4: K2, yo, k1, yo, k2.

Row 6: K3, yo, k1, yo, k3.

Row 8: Ssk, k5, k2tog.

Row 10: Ssk, k3, k2tog.

Row 12: Ssk, k1, k2tog.

Row 14: Slip 1, k2tog, pass slipped st over next. Break yarn.

fringe

Measure out and set aside approx 1 yd. of yarn for seaming handles and leaf after felting. Then, cut the rest of the yarn into 9-in. lengths for fringe.

Attach fringe all along front flap using a crochet hook.

construction and felting

Keep the bag, leaf, and handle separate while you felt.

Put bag in a pillowcase and felt in the washing machine with a few towels, or felt by hand.

A note on washing machines

If you do put your bag in the washer, make sure you check on it from time to time to rip apart the fringes if they start to stick together. Mine did, and I had to rip and cut at them a bit! Yes I almost cried, but then I worked at it and shaped it until it looked pretty again. It's amazing what the finishing touches do to a felting project. Don't give up if it comes out all wobbly-like at first. Patient shaping is key.

After bag, leaf, and handle are felted down to desired size, shape them and set them flat to dry. I curved the leaf at the tip a bit and put knitting needles of graduating sizes in the holes to keep them open while it dried.

finishing

Take the handle and twist it until it folds in half upon itself. Stitch to either side of the inside of bag.

Attach the leaf to the side of the bag by the felted tail at the base. (I attached a few bells as well.)

Stitch the button to the front. Weave and trim all ends.

Now you are ready to stack your favorite novels into your magic treetop bag and climb the nearest tree. Hang the bag from a branch and watch it sway in the breeze as you flip through the pages.

SLEEPING BEAUTY

Sleeping beauty has it all: a nice soft bed, the scent of roses gently lofting through her bedroom window, and a perfect excuse to sleep in. "Hey guys, I'm sorry I missed the meeting. See, I was under this spell . . . "

experience level
Intermediate

Very basic crochet skills needed

size
One size, adult average

measurements
6 in. tall and 13 in. wide at bottom edge, laid flat

yarn
• Approx 250 yd. worsted weight yarn (CYCA 4)

• Approx 145 yd. DK weight yarn (CYCA 3)

• Scraps of yellow or pink yarn

shown in
• Dream in Color Classy: 100% superwash merino wool (250 yd./229 m, 4 oz./ 113 g), 1 skein in Vino Veritas (MC)

• The Fibre Company Acadia: 60% merino, 20% silk, 20% alpaca (145 yd./133 m, 1.75 oz./50 g), 1 skein Sea Lavender (CC)

gauge
21 sts = 4 in. in chart pattern using U.S. size 6 (4 mm) needles and worsted weight yarn.

notions
• One U.S. size 6 (4 mm) circular needle 16 in. long (or size necessary for gauge; see Note)

• Size H (4.5 mm) crochet hook

• Size F (3.75 mm) crochet hook

• Stitch marker

• Tapestry needle

• 2 yd. of black shirring elastic

Note: This yarn normally calls for a needle as small as U.S. size 7. However, as this pattern has lots of ribbing, I went down a needle size to U.S. size 6 to get a nice tight look. Please use needles necessary for you to get the correct gauge.

PATTERN NOTES

The cowl starts at the bottom and is knitted in the round. The top of the neck is lightly cinched with shirring elastic instead of a bind-off. Roses and forget-me-nots are crocheted separately and attached at the end.

tiny owl stitch gauge

See p. 30 for abbreviations.

to make cowl

The pattern repeat is a multiple of 14 sts.

With MC and size 6 circular needle, CO 126 sts, pm, and join in the round. Rep instructions in [ ] below.

Round 1: [K2, p1, k1, p1, k2, p7] to end.

Round 2: [K2, pfb, kb, pfb, k2, p2tog, p3, p2tog] to end.

Round 3: [K2, p2, k1, p2, k2, p5] to end.

Round 4: [K2, pfb, p1, kb, p1, pfb, k2, p2tog, p1, p2tog] to end.

Round 5: [K2, p3, k1, p3, k2, p3] to end.

Round 6: [K2, p3, MK, p3, k2, p1, kb, p1] to end.

Round 7: [K2, p7, k2, p1, k1, p1] to end.

Round 8: [K2, p2tog, p3, p2tog, k2, pfb, kb, pfb] to end.

Round 9: [K2, p5, k2, p2, k1, p2]

Round 10: [K2, p2tog, p1, p2tog, k2, pfb, p1, kb, p1, pfb] to end.

Round 11: [K2, p3, k2, p3, k1, p3] to end.

Round 12: [K2, p1, kb, p1, k2, p3 MK, p3] to end.

Work Rounds 1–12 completely a total of 2 times. Then work Round 1 again. Don't bind off.

finishing the cowl

Thread tapestry needle with 2 yd. of shirring elastic held tripled. Slip the "live" stitches off the knitting needle and onto the shirring elastic. Yeah, it's unconventional, but I promise it is secure! The elastic keeps sts in shape, and the yarn is so spongy, you won't even be able to see it. Slip the cowl over your head before tying the elastic in a knot. Make sure that the elastic is comfortably snug on your neck, but that you can still get the cowl on and off without trouble. Don't forget to weave the final yarn tail, too.

red roses

(Make 9)

With MC and H crochet hook, loosely ch 12, turn.

Row 1: * Dc into 2nd ch from hook, work 2 dc into that same st, then work 3 dc into each st across. Turn. **Important:** Take time to mark this as your right side. It will be the side facing out when you roll the rose into a spiral.

Row 2: Ch 2, work 2 dc into each st across.

Break yarn, leaving a long tail for sewing the flower. Roll the ruffle into a spiral shape with the right side facing out, and you will see a flower appear. Do a few simple straight stitches into the flower to secure it into shape.

little blue forget-me-nots

(Make 9)

With CC and size F crochet hook, ch 4, slip st into 1st ch to form ring.

Round 1: Ch 2, 8 dc into ring, join with slip st into top of ch 2.

Break yarn, pull tail through center. Weave the 2 tails into the ring securely to hide them.

It is not necessary to sleep while wearing this cowl. You may have much better success with it if you wear it while you are awake!

finishing

Attaching the roses

Notice that you have 9 pattern repeats in your cowl. There are enough roses to space them out evenly. I arranged the roses so they were at the bottom center of each "open hour-glass" shape. This particular placement isn't crucial; it's just nice to have the roses stay clear of covering up the little knot bobbles.

Placement tip: Align the very center of each rose with the very edge of the cowl. Do a few simple tacking sts to secure each rose around the bottom edges of the cowl. You may want to work a st to tack the edges of the rose down, too.

Attaching the forget-me-nots

Use some yellow yarn to attach the forget-me-nots to the cowl in between each rose.

Tie the ends in a double knot in the center of the flower and trim ends to make the little stamens.

TINY OWL STITCH GUIDE

beg: beginning

CC: contrasting color

CO: cast on. Casting on in the middle of a row is easy; just make a simple backward loop with your thumb and slide it onto the right needle.

c2b: slip next st onto cable needle purlwise and hold to back of work, knit next st, knit st from cable needle.

c2f: slip next st onto cable needle purlwise and hold to front of work, knit next st, knit st from cable needle.

dec: decrease(s)

dpns: double-pointed needles

foll: follows/following

k: knit

kb: knit into the back of the next st

knitwise: go into st as if to knit

kfb: knit into front and back of st

k2tog: knit the next 2 sts together

mb: knit into front and back and front of st, turn. Purl 3, turn. K1, k2tog, and pass knit st over (one bobble made).

MC: main color

m1: lift up the bar before the next stitch front to back and place on the left needle, knit into the back of st.

m1p: lift up the bar before the next st and place it on left needle, purl into back of st.

MK: make knot. (K1, p1, k1, p1, k1) loosely into next st, then slip the first 4 of these sts one at a time over the final knit st made.

p: purl

pm: place marker

pull up loop: insert the point of the right needle upward under the 2 strands in front of the slip sts and knit the next st off the left needle. Then lift the 2 strands up and over the point of the right needle.

purlwise: go into st as if to purl

p2tog: purl the next 2 sts together

pfb: purl into the front and back of next st

RS: right side

rem: remaining

rep: repeat

rm: remove marker

skp: slip 1 st as if to knit, knit the next st, pass the slipped st over the knit st.

sm: slip marker

St st: stockinette st. Knit a row, purl a row.

st(s): stitch(es)

ssk: slip next 2 sts knitwise onto your right needle, insert left needle purlwise into the front of the sts and knit them together.

t2b: slip next st onto cable needle purlwise and hold to back of work, knit next st, purl st from cable needle.

t2f: slip next st onto cable needle purlwise and hold to front of work, purl next st, knit st from cable needle.

WS: wrong side

yo: yarn over. Start with yarn at back of work. Bring yarn between needles and then back over the right needle.

CROCHET STITCHES

ch: chain

dc: double crochet

ss: slip stitch

RESOURCES

Etsy.com

Specialty yarns and other crafting supplies.

Jo-Ann Fabrics and Craft Stores®

www.joann.com

Yarn, notions, and crafting supplies

Michaels®

www.michaels.com

Yarn, notions, and other crafting supplies.

Walmart

www.walmart.com

Yarns, notions, and other crafting supplies.

STANDARD YARN WEIGHTS

NUMBERED BALL	DESCRIPTION	STS/4 IN.	NEEDLE SIZE
1 SUPER FINE	Sock, baby, fingering	27–32	2.25–3.25 mm (U.S. 1–3)
2 FINE	Sport, baby	23–26	3.25–3.75 mm (U.S. 3–5)
3 LIGHT	DK, light worsted	21–24	3.75–4.5 mm (U.S. 5–7)
4 MEDIUM	Worsted, afghan, Aran	16–20	4.5–5.5 mm (U.S. 7–9)
5 BULKY	Chunky, craft, rug	12–15	5.5–8.0 mm (U.S. 9–11)
6 SUPER BULKY	Bulky, roving	6–11	8 mm and larger (U.S. 11 and larger)